QUEEN CHRISTINA

by Pam Gems

QUEEN CHRISTINA

a play in two acts

by Pam Gems

St. Luke's Press
23-25 Kensington Park Road
London W.11

CAUTION

All rights whatsoever in this play are strictly reserved and applications for performance, professional or amateur, must be made, in advance, to ACTAC Ltd., 16 Cadogan Lane, London, S.W.1. Tel: 01-235-2797

First published in 1982 by St. Luke's Press
23-25 Kensington Park Road London W11
Printed by

Vectis Lithographics Ltd;
Newport & Ryde, Isle of Wight

ISBN 0 9508443 0 6

© *1982 by Pam Gems*

Second Edition

QUEEN CHRISTINA

CHRONOLOGY OF THE LIFE OF THE REAL
QUEEN CHRISTINA

1626   Birth of CHRISTINA
1632   Death of her father, KING GUSTAVUS ADOLPHUS
1644   CHRISTINA comes of age
1648   Peace of Westphalia, the end of the Thirty Years War
1649   The succession of PRINCE KARL GUSTAV confirmed
1650   DESCARTES visits Sweden *(and dies there)*
1650   Coronation of QUEEN CHRISTINA
1654   Abdication of QUEEN CHRISTINA
1655   CHRISTINA confirmed as a Roman Catholic in St. Peter's
1656   CHRISTINA attempts to secure the throne of Naples
1657   Death of MONALDESCHO
1658   CHRISTINA returns to Rome
1666   CHRISTINA bids for the Polish crown
1689   CHRISTINA dies

QUEEN CHRISTINA was written in 1975. The play is not a documentary, thus characters have been concertinaed, and some events changed. All plays are metaphors, and the dilemma of the real CHRISTINA, reared and educated as a man for the Swedish throne, and then asked to marry and breed for the succession, is perhaps not irrelevant today.

QUEEN CHRISTINA was first produced by The Royal Shakespeare Company at The Other Place, Stratford-upon-Avon, in October, 1977. The cast was as follows:

QUEEN CHRISTINA	Sheila Allen
CHRISTINA, as a child	Erin Tyler
CHANCELLOR AXEL OXENSTIERNA	Bernard Brown
KING GUSTAVUS ADOLPHUS	Barrie Rutter
GERMAN PRINCE	Iain Mitchell
GERMAN AMBASSADOR	John Burgess
LADY EBBA SPARRE	Charlotte Cornwell
QUEEN MOTHER	Valerie Lush
DESCARTES	John Burgess
MAGNUS DE LA GUARDIE	Nigel Terry
PRINCE KARL	Ian McNeice
GIRL	Fleur Chandler
CHANUT	Barrie Rutter
SECRETARY	Iain Mitchell
COPLEMAN	Nigel Terry
DUKE	Iain Mitchell
BISHOP	John Burgess
MARQUISE	Valerie Lush
MARIANNE	Fleur Chandler
CATHERINE DE ROHANT	Charlotte Cornwell
COUNT OF BREVAYE	Iain Mitchell
POPE	Bernard Brown
MONALDESCHO	Nigel Terry
CARDINAL AZZOLINO	Ian McNeice
CAPTAIN	John Burgess
SOLDIER	Barrie Rutter
LUCIA	Valerie Lush

ANGELICA, as a child	Erin Tyler
ANGELICA	Fleur Chandler
RUFFINO	Iain Mitchell
ROMANO	Barrie Rutter
SALVATORE	Nigel Terry
MUSICIAN	Robin Weatherall

Directed by Penny Cherns
Designed by Di Seymour
Music by Guy Woolfenden
Lighting by Leo Leibovici
Choreography by Gillian Lynne
Fight directed by Nick Stringer
Company voice work by Cicely Berry

DIRECTOR of THE OTHER PLACE   Ron Daniels

QUEEN CHRISTINA

CAST

CHRISTINA
KING
AXEL
CHILD
PRINCE
AMBASSADOR
PRINCE KARL
MAGNUS
EBBA
QUEEN MOTHER
CHANUT
GIRL
DUKE
COPLEMAN
BISHOP
MARQUISE
CATHERINE
POPE
CARDINALS
MONALDESCHO
AZZOLINO
CAPTAIN
SOLDIER
LUCIA
ANGELICA

The play may be performed with a cast of three women, five men and a child.

ACT ONE

SCENE ONE

Succession

A SMALL CHILD *crouches in a huge fireplace, lit by the glow from the fire.* TWO MEN, *one dressed as a soldier, pace. Off, there is screaming, ending in a howl of pain.* AXEL OXENSTIERNA, *Chancellor, exits. He returns after a brief pause. The* KING *looks across at him bleakly. As bleakly, he shakes his head.*

KING	Dead?
AXEL	As before.
KING	Was it a boy?
AXEL	I believe so.
KING	How is she?
AXEL	Losing blood.
KING	What is it with women? Weak!

The QUEEN *begins to sob, and the low sobbing continues throughout the scene.*

AXEL	There's always next year.
KING	If she breeds again it'll finish her, I'm surprised she's alive this time.
AXEL	I'm sorry. If it weren't for the succession ...
KING	I'm well aware.
AXEL	What about the Palatinate alliance .. good strong girl ..
KING	We have a queen – godammit man, she's not dead yet. *(He moves away, notices the child)* We do *have* an heir. *(Gestures the child)*

AXEL	A girl.
KING	She's fit enough. Intelligent.
AXEL	But the wrong sex! With a weak succession it'll be anybody's game, we can't have a woman.
KING	Make a man of her then.
AXEL	How?
KING	Training.

Pause.

AXEL	I'd need legislation for that.
KING	Draft it. *(Looks at the child)* I want her fit, educated, able to lead an army if necessary.
AXEL	We'll talk about it later.
KING	No. I shall be with the army tomorrow – God knows when we'll meet again.
AXEL	Just the thing for you.
KING	Yes. All this howling, I'd rather face a brigade of guards. Make a man of her, for my sake.

They clasp hands. The KING puts on his gloves.

AXEL	I'm sorry, sir.
KING	Yes, I thought a son this time. *(Looks at the child)* She'd better live with you. I'll tell the Queen.

AXEL bows and leaves. The KING turns to the child.

	What did you think of that .. were you listening?
CHILD	Why is Mama crying?
KING	We're going to make a queen of you.

CHILD   *(flinches)* No, I don't want to.
KING   Don't worry, not like your mother .. like me,
                 like a king. You'll be living with the Chancellor
                 from now on. Do as he says, and be good, for
                 my sake. Oh, and try not to fidget in church ..
                 we mustn't upset the Lutherans.

He lifts and kisses her. She throws her arms about his neck and won't let go.

CHILD   Don't leave me here.

He prises her off, sets her down.

KING   A king must fight. Now remember, look after
                 your mother. Take care of her, she's a woman.

He makes to go in one direction, then turns and exits towards the sound of sobbing. The CHILD moves after him, then stops. She hugs her doll.

AXEL enters and stands apart, frowning at her. She looks back, and they appraise each other with level stares.

SCENE TWO

Betrothal

The SWEDISH PALACE. *A bare, bleak interior.*

Enter a GERMAN PRINCE, *a small man, waiting to be received as a suitor. He wears Swedish ribbons on each shoulder. He is followed by* AXEL, *now grizzled, who is talking to the Prince's* AMBASSADOR.

AMBASSADOR As I say, we are fully empowered to negotiate.

AXEL Good. Good. We might even touch on trade talks .. if it's within the brief.

AMBASSADOR The visit of your ambassadors to the Flemish court has been noted.

AXEL Oh, purely formal. Fishing rights, that sort of thing.

AMBASSADOR Glad to have your assurance. Of course .. everything depends .. *(He looks toward the* PRINCE*)* ... His Royal Highness was most impressed with the miniature. We hear nothing but the most glowing reports of Her Majesty's beauty.

AXEL *(neutral)* What?

AMBASSADOR It will greatly facilitate negotiations if .. if ah ... *(He smiles, waggish, at* AXEL, *who returns a gloomy stare)* if the royal consorts .. ah ...

PRINCE He means if we fancy each other. Absolutely, you bet .. I'm a man of feeling, Chancellor.

AXEL I trust Your Royal Highness has the interests of your country at heart.

PRINCE Of course. Oh don't worry, we know the score ... the hard work you chaps have put in on behalf of .. of ...

AMBASSADOR Of a fruitful and enduring relationship between our two great nations.

PRINCE Right. Speaking of which, where is the wench?

AXEL Her Majesty always hunts before breakfast, Sire. Perhaps your Highness would care to inspect the Flemish tapestries.

PRINCE Bugger the Flemish tapestries, I've been here an hour, we're getting into protocol!

AMBASSADOR Patience, Sire. Never known a woman to
                be on time, eh Chancellor?
AXEL   What? Oh, here they are. *(He sounds
                surprised).*

*A beautiful young woman enters. She is wearing a simple but
beautifully cut riding habit. Her pale ringlets fall about a
beautiful but thoughtful face. She smiles as she approaches,
and the* PRINCE, *enchanted, moves forward, smiling in
delight.*

MAN   *(at the door)* What's all this?

*He enters, a battered figure in hunting clothes. He slouches up
to the young woman, moving louchely .. he appears to be
slightly crippled, or perhaps it is that one of his shoulders is out
of true, giving him a swivelled, crooked appearance. He puts a
familiar hand on the young woman's shoulder.*

                Who the hell's this?

The PRINCE, *deeply insulted, nonetheless steps forward to
present himself. The* MAN *bursts out laughing. The* PRINCE
puts his hand to his sword, glaring at AXEL, *who stands grim
and unmoving. Nonplussed, the* PRINCE *kisses the young
woman's hand with a flourish.*

MAN   Steady on .. steady on!

                The PRINCE *is now totally affronted.*

PRINCE   *(through his teeth to his ambassador)* Do
                something!

The AMBASSADOR *whispers to him, agitated and placating.*

MAN	*(to* AXEL*).* Who is it?
AXEL	*(through his teeth)* It's the royal suitor! Put up your sword, man – *(as the* PRINCE, *outraged at the man's snigger, draws his sword)*
PRINCE	I see .. I see! So this is our future consort ... trailing a fellow about her like a common .. a common ...
AMBASSADOR	Sire ..
PRINCE	It's outrageous .. bloody outrageous ....
MAN	At least there's some spunk in him. *(He thumps the* PRINCE *genially on the shoulder, sending him reeling, then turns to* AXEL *with a murderous face)* Some sort of joke?
AXEL	You've been fully aware of the negotiations.
MAN	And you're developing a sense of humour.
AXEL	May I remind you that we are talking of royal connection – this is not a personal area.
MAN	And may I remind you that there is a limit. For God's sake, man.. I mean – look!

He .. she .. that is to say, CHRISTINA, *takes the* PRINCE'S *nerveless arm and stands beside him in wifely stance. Even* AXEL *masks a momentary smile.*

CHRISTINA	You'll have to do better than this. I'm sorry, little fellow.
AMBASSADOR	*(faintly)* Are we .. are we to understand ...?
AXEL	You are in the presence of Her Majesty.

CHRISTINA   Nothing like a formal introduction. I suppose
             they've been showing you some fancy-assed
             painting – think yourself lucky we weren't
             married off by proxy – oh, get rid of them,
             Axel, I've taken one fall already this morning.
             There is one matter. *(They pause)* No more
             Swedish troops. You can have a few forests
             instead ... believe me, timber lasts longer. *(to*
             AXEL, *hard)* See to it.

She bows the visitors out with courtesy. AXEL *glares and
goes.*

EBBA   You've upset him.
CHRISTINA   He'll get his own back.
EBBA   You're well-matched.
CHRISTINA   Not surprising – I'm his boy. Sending me
             notes to dress up like a monkey's arse.
EBBA   You knew perfectly well they were coming.
CHRISTINA   And what they were after. I'll end this bloody
             war if it's the – ahh! *(She groans, pressing her
             abdomen).* My bloody period. Of all the
             ludicrous patterns in nature, hens are better
             off.
MOTHER   *(off)* .... let me pass, I know she's in there ..
CHRISTINA   Quick, get rid of her.

EBBA *shakes her head helplessly as* CHRISTINA'S
MOTHER *enters. She is fine-boned, dressed in messy finery.
She presents the picture of an intensely unhappy woman, near
anguish. She is often coarse, trivial, out of place, even comic.
But the intensity of unhappiness, and her bewilderment,
prevent us from finding her just a figure of fun. A beautiful
woman who has now lost her looks.*

MOTHER	There you are .. there you are! Why do you keep avoiding us? *(Curtseys .. waits)* If we don't sit down we shall scream.
CHRISTINA	*(motions her to sit)* Not too upset to forget the royal we, you notice.
MOTHER	Turned you down, has he?
CHRISTINA	Other way round!
MOTHER	Took one look, couldn't run fast enough, well don't blame me. *(to EBBA)* What did he say, is he off?

EBBA *turns away, with a look at* CHRISTINA.

	.. oh, I should know better than to ask her. I saw you in the stables this morning, the pair of you. At least I could get a man.
CHRISTINA	What do you want?
MOTHER	Nothing you can give me. Oh, what does she look like? All those babies, and she had to be the one to live!
CHRISTINA	*(scuffles across, jerking her crippled shoulder at her mother)* Did your best to do me in, crippled me for life.
MOTHER	Stop it! .. the nurse dropped you! Anyway, what difference does it make, you're so ugly –
CHRISTINA	As you never tire of telling me.
MOTHER	It's true! *(Weeps)* I'm not staying in this hellhole another winter, I shall go to Italy.
CHRISTINA	Clear off, the sooner the better.
MOTHER	What? But we shan't see you then!
CHRISTINA	Good.
MOTHER	But we're your mother!
CHRISTINA	*(doubles in pain)* Ohh!
MOTHER	I've a right to grandchildren, the same as any

	other woman – what's the matter, can't you bear to look at us?
EBBA	Her Majesty is not well this morning.
MOTHER	What?
EBBA	*(leading the* QUEEN MOTHER *off)* She's very tense.
MOTHER	Tense? What's she got to be tense about? Wait till you're my age, ignored, no pension, treated without respect – wait till you've got wrinkles on your face, see how much notice they take of you then! Tense! When have I had a night's rest with the neuralgia .. EBBA *steers her out, returns.*
CHRISTINA	Ugh.
EBBA	You know what she wants.
CHRISTINA	Money.
EBBA	She wants your love.
CHRISTINA	What! You've had your hair done.
EBBA	I was wondering when you'd notice. It's still damp, do you like it?
CHRISTINA	You look like a young birch tree. Oh!

She dives at EBBA *roughly, going for her breasts like an importunate baby.* EBBA *lets her nurse briefly.* CHRISTINA *becomes calmer.*

EBBA	You were cruel – no I mean it, Pixie.
CHRISTINA	Hah, seen the new casualty lists?
EBBA	Yes.
CHRISTINA	Thirty years at war. Now they want me to breed for it.
EBBA	Why *NOT* Prince Karl? At least as your cousin he's in the family.

CHRISTINA *(absently)* Be like fucking your own sword handle. What sort of litter do you think we'd produce, by God, when I'm with you I forget, *you* become my mirror, I see *your* face, *your* eyes.

EBBA Beauty isn't everything.

CHRISTINA Isn't it? I hear you've got a new beau. *(EBBA is startled, as* CHRISTINA *has intended)* Is he handsome?

EBBA Yes. May I present him?

CHRISTINA All right, but don't love him too much. *(Walks)*. Christian war! .. connote me that phrase. Yesterday we hanged five boys – ah, says Axel, when order's restored we can relax the severity. Who shall we *BE* when we've killed and mutilated half Sweden?

EBBA No-one blames you.

CHRISTINA They should.

EBBA It's your duty.

CHRISTINA Another word of unfathomable meaning.

EBBA Pixie why go against the grain? Play by the rules, you are still free to think.

CHRISTINA Live like a toad under a stone? And since when have you had a reflective nature .. I saw your eyes on the boys last night.

EBBA If you did you shouldn't have – *I* don't care to show.

CHRISTINA Except to me.

EBBA Except to you, of course.

CHRISTINA I love you.

EBBA I know.

CHRISTINA I often wonder what you think about that.

EBBA I'm honoured.

CHRISTINA   Is that all? Don't punish me. Why should I endure her? I tell you, I begin to find endurance insufficient.

EBBA   It is hard.

CHRISTINA   No, it's too easy, that's the trouble! Oh Belle. Why are we given life? In order to suffer.. to be stoic? If so, why the larch tree? Why you? I think! To what purpose? For to believe we're here *because* .. or *in order to* – why that's to accept the most horrifying malignancy or the unbelievably inept! Pestilence ... the murder of children – by design? Better no meaning at all, I begin not to believe in anything ... oh, don't worry, I keep it to myself. Still, no doubt about it – the idea of a First Cause begins to look like a Swiss cheese.

EBBA   What?

CHRISTINA   The notion of the Creation, my dear, has acquired a distinct wobble. D'you know what they're saying?

EBBA   No.

CHRISTINA   They are saying.. that the earth is round ... and hangs, like a ball, in space.

EBBA   Nonsense! Oh, you read too much! Christina life is for living! Life! We must live!

CHRISTINA   Well, we'll see what our Monsieur Descartes has to make of it.

EBBA   I insist that you dress up for him. We can't have a Frenchman putting us out of face.

CHRISTINA   That little man's going to unlock doors for me or I'll kick him for a fraud.

EBBA   What about the Italian dress? *(she runs off)*

CHRISTINA   No.

She walks, restless. Catches her reflection in the glass.

> Even my bitch is in love. You fool, take your
> pick. He'll come unwilling either way so
> choose the best pair of legs in Europe.
>
> There must be someone willing to prance with
> me.
>
> No man who wants a person?
>
> No such luck.

She turns abruptly and leaves. EBBA *enters, the dress over her
arm.* MAGNUS DE LA GUARDIE, *young and handsome,
enters separately.*
*They glance to make sure that they are not observed and
embrace briefly.*

MAGNUS	When? When?
EBBA	Not yet .. we must be careful. I'll catch her in the right mood.

They go. Blackout.

SCENE THREE

Welcome, Monsieur Descartes

*A chair for the Queen, another for the Queen Mother, seats for
Axel and Descartes.*

Enter the QUEEN MOTHER. *She is eating from a large,
ornate box of chocolates.* DESCARTES *attends her, followed
by* AXEL.

MOTHER	Chocolate, Mossoo Desscart?
DESCARTES	Thank you, gracious madame, but no.
MOTHER	They're soft centres, from Prague!
DESCARTES	*(disguising a belch)*. I have been fed most .. royally at your table.
MOTHER	Yes, nice piece of cow, we enjoyed it. Of course, meat isn't at its best this time of year, but with a few turnips, and a boiled potato –
AXEL	*(Sourly)*. Her Majesty enjoys her food.
MOTHER	What else is there for me to enjoy? I still miss him, you know, Mossoo … my lovely husband. I have his clothes put out every night. *(She dives into her bosom and fetches out a miniature)*. His likeness! Pretty man, doncha think?
DESCARTES	A noble countenance.
MOTHER	Split clean down the middle on the field.
DESCARTES	Chere Madame!
MOTHER	He'd eat a side of beef for starters – well, you have to keep out the cold in this icehole.
DESCARTES	A most beautiful man.

THE QUEEN MOTHER *kicks her dwarf who presents the box she carries to* DESCARTES, *who assumes it to be a gift.*

	My most gracious thanks, madame.
MOTHER	*(peals of laughter)*. Oh, it's not for you! He thinks it's for him, what a gaffe Monsieur, never mind, we forgive you. You can have a look.

She watches fondly as he opens the lid.

We never go anywhere without it.

DESCARTES *looks inside, claps the lid shut.*

> There! What do you think of that! The heart and member of a King! I bet you've never seen that before.

DESCARTES *shakes his head weakly.*

> I've precious little else, Mossoo, a woman in my position has no-one to protect her. Tell me, are you a married man yourself?

AXEL *(heavy)* I think the dance is about to begin.

CHRISTINA *hisses and gestures. They sit. Loud gigglings and whisperings, off, then* CHRISTINA *erupts onto the scene. She is wearing a costume and looks like nothing on earth.*

CHRISTINA My Lords and Ladies ... in honour of Monsieur Descartes, our distinguished guest .. we present ... our Masque! I shall play –

MOTHER What's it about?

CHRISTINA War and peace, I keep telling you! I shall play Peace. I am Peace. Magnus is War – Magnus ..

MAGNUS *enters.*

> The part of War is played by our friend Duke Magnus de la Guardie. *(She gives him a kiss)*

MOTHER He's only a Duke.

CHRISTINA Belle! (EBBA *enters)* The Lady Ebba Sparre plays Venus ... ooh! *(She gives* EBBA *a hug and a kiss)* Oh and there's Karl. What's Karl playing, Magnus?

MAGNUS Sweden, Ma'am.

CHRISTINA   Yes, he's Sweden, the Swedish people, that sort of thing. I play Peace. Right, we'll start. Mars, the God of War, descends on the people. Venus tries to help but that's no good. Then I come on and peace conquers all.

Music. The Masque begins. The QUEEN MOTHER *provides a running commentary, to* CHRISTINA'S *wrath.*

MOTHER   *(as* KARL, *with clumsy good will, does his dance)* Oh Karl! Oh, isn't he good! *(On* MARS' *galvanic entrance)* Ooh, oh, ooh! *(Clutching* DESCARTES *for protection)* Oh Mossoo .. oh, poor Sweden! Ahhh!! *(As* EBBA *descends, trailing draperies)* Oh, isn't she sweet ... so pretty ... how enchanting! Oh dear. *(As* CHRISTINA *makes her entrance)* Oh. Oh well, never mind.

The Masque ends in a gigue. It becomes a romp as CHRISTINA, *breaking the steps, twirls with* MAGNUS. *She shrieks with pleasure as the music ends, throwing her arms about* MAGNUS' *neck.*

CHRISTINA   *(reeling)* Anyone would think we were drunk!

MAGNUS *crosses swiftly, whispers to* EBBA.

EBBA   No please .. not yet!

MAGNUS *whispers briefly to* AXEL.

CHRISTINA   Come on, no whispering – by God, what a handsome fellow!

MAGNUS   A mere shank to the pearl of Your Majesty's
            radiance.
CHRISTINA   Get off, you sound like a Frenchman .. oops,
            sorry!   My two dear friends! *(she embraces
            them)* Where's the brandy, we'll put some fire
            in your feet, little philosopher .. did you like
            the painting? *(Throws herself on the throne)*
DESCARTES   My thanks again, Majesty. Your Majesty has
            a marvellous eye!
CHRISTINA   Surprised eh? Not much culture in this cold
            country. We've another for you.
MOTHER   She's been spending again.
CHRISTINA   Why not? No point of we can't share our love,
            eh Magnus?
AXEL   Your Majesty is in a mood for good news.
CHRISTINA   Look at him, sober as a judge .. yes, come on,
            let's have it man. And give us a smile, melt the
            Pole!
AXEL   I ask your formal permission for a projected
            marriage.
CHRISTINA   *(intense suspicion)* Marriage? What have you
            been up to, Karl?
KARL   Nothing, cousin, I assure you.
AXEL   I make formal request, for the betrothal of two
            of your most devoted subjects.
CHRISTINA   Splendid, who is it?
AXEL   We ask your formal consent to the marriage of
            the Lady Ebba Sparre with the Duke Magnus
            de la Guardie.

Silence. Then CHRISTINA *lurches to her feet. She glares,
then begins to screech, becoming hysterical.*

CHRISTINA   Bitch ... bitch! Liars .. cheats!

MOTHER   You see? You see? It's always the same!

CHRISTINA   Vicious, hateful cow!

KARL *tries to restrain her.*

CHRISTINA   Get off, you fat fool .. get off! *She grapples
with him, clouting him savagely and pulling
his hair. Everyone seeks to go, but she hauls
DESCARTES back, clinging to him for a
second. He waits, while she howls and sobs.
She throws herself down on her throne at last,
sniffing, and blowing her nose loudly in her
skirt. She becomes aware of his presence and
flinches. Pause.*

CHRISTINA   *(mutters)* Good of you to sit with us.

DESCARTES The honour is mine.

CHRISTINA   I've made a fool of myself. We were hoping to
impress you with our qualities of mind.

DESCARTES Your Majesty is young. You bear a special
burden.

CHRISTINA   Yet who more privileged? Most people
struggle for mere existence. Don't you find
that inept – that the most suffer the most?

DESCARTES It is a puzzle.

CHRISTINA   Then you imply solution. I wish I had access to
it .. by God, I can't even secure my own
happiness. Am I, in my privilege, to derive
contentment solely from the nourishment of
others? Do you not consider that to be unjust?
And, if unjust, does it not call for action?

DESCARTES If the action be just.

CHRISTINA   Good, I'll have his head for it.

DESCARTES Can the road to happiness lie thus?

CHRISTINA Be careful, I'm not in the mood for the cold shale of endurance.

DESCARTES Madame, there is choice.

CHRISTINA Choice? Hah. Between circumstance and the flesh we are all slaves.

DESCARTES In part. We know that we must die. Which does not absolve us from the challenge of choosing.

CHRISTINA The making of decision, little Frenchman, is my daily burden.

DESCARTES But with choice there is possibility. For change. And the concept of change implies the very world within our grasp. It is we who decide.

CHRISTINA *(Pause)* You may be right. *(She chews her nails)* I loved him. I let him see that I loved him, they all saw that I loved him. Now tell me how he can live.

DESCARTES Through the mercy of princes.

CHRISTINA *(groans)* And how do I survive? *(She stands, and begins to shake uncontrollably)* How ... how?

DESCARTES Perhaps, in the end, we must learn to love those things we *CAN* have.

CHRISTINA *groans again.*

CHRISTINA Tell me how to live! I cannot go forward to the next moment in my life!

DESCARTES Pain passes.

CHRISTINA All very well for you, little philosopher. You tip the world on its head and leave the rest of us to reset the pieces. It's we who decide, is it? Can't see the priests approving of that. Well, we'll talk again. *(He bows, dismissed, makes to go)* And wrap up warmly. We don't want the world saying Sweden finished you off. *(He bows again, goes)*

Yes, well ... a man .. a philosopher. Runs down a pink road while the world gets the wheat in. What about me, the worms in my belly? Coming to me with the salt of a man on her, swearing her love – what do you want? *(As KARL enters and coughs politely. She crosses to him, flicks the ribbons on his shoulders)* What's this, the ribbons of a suitor, Karl?

KARL   Forgive me, I must speak.

CHRISTINA   Don't presume too far on old acquaintance.

KARL   I want you to know that I'm here.

CHRISTINA   Clever timing. The popular solution. Our feelings, of course, are irrelevant.

KARL   I think you know mine.

CHRISTINA   What?

KARL   I said, I think you know mine, Christina. I can understand that I don't please you. I'm not well-favoured.

CHRISTINA   What am I supposed to say .. that we're not a pair of uglies? The flies will fall off the wall on our wedding night, there isn't a tavern joke I haven't thought of already.

KARL   I do so love your vicious intelligence.

CHRISTINA   Yes, well, that almost reached me. Possibilities. Perverse, of course, but then you always did like me beating you up. *(She grabs his hair, as before)*

KARL   I'm sorry, I don't know what you mean.

CHRISTINA   No, you wouldn't – oh, clear off. For Christ's sake, what is there in my fat face that gives you a tremble?

KARL   I wish you wouldn't. Christina, you have such a wonderful countenance. I never tire of the wit and life in your eyes. And did you know .. you have very pretty ears.

CHRISTINA   Ears? What sort of fool d'you take me for? Ears? You – are fat. Your lips pout like a girls, your legs are bandy and you walk with your ass cocked up like a turkey. What makes you think I could fancy a squat little asshole like you? I've got the pick of Europe! *(Her voice breaks, she turns away)*

KARL   *(pause)* You *CAN* trust me.

CHRISTINA   That's true.

KARL   Then you consent?

CHRISTINA   It's all the same to me. I suppose so.

KARL   Oh, Christina, if you knew how I loved you!

CHRISTINA   What? We'll have none of that.

KARL   But I mean it. I love you!

CHRISTINA   Love? You? Do you think I want to be desired by the likes of you? A man who fancies a long-nosed cripple? Since there's no sap of ambition in you, and I doubt you've the wit for contrivance, it must be aberration!

KARL   Christina ..

CHRISTINA   Get away!

KARL   Christina, please ..

CHRISTINA   No! There's one freak on the throne .. no need to perpetuate the joke. The answer's no.

Pause. Then he bows and goes. CHRISTINA *paces, then sits.*

CHRISTINA   *(pause)* What do they mean ... a ball hanging in space?

It's almost imaginative.

A pause.

Why not? Make a widower of him tonight? Tell him to shut his eyes and call me Belle? Two sons and a thousand gifts later he won't even remember the difference.

Why not?

She breaks briefly, then recovers herself.

One. Create Karl Commander in Chief of the Army. Two. Make Magnus ambassador to Paris. Give, Christina, give, give! And watch your position. Guard the throne. It's all you have.

She goes.

SCENE FOUR

A Warm Wind From The South

CHRISTINA'S BEDCHAMBER. *The bedcurtains drawn. The* QUEEN MOTHER *sits by the bed huddled in fur and sheepskins. Still cold she pulls the rug from the floor over her knees.*

AXEL *enters with a scroll.*

MOTHER	She's ill.
AXEL	I am assured that Her Majesty is well enough to receive me. Pray inform her.
MOTHER	Certainly not. If you approach the Queen's bed we shall call the guard and have you arrested for an attack on the Queen's person.
AXEL	Madam, will you return to your embroideries and not try my patience.
MOTHER	Oh yes, wouldn't you love to get your hands on me.
AXEL	Hardly, madam.
MOTHER	Oh? Times have changed! Where's the notorious straying hand? The last time was in Church, and it was Lent.
AXEL	I must have been drunk.
MOTHER	*(gloomily)* You were too incapable to do anything. I suppose it's young flesh you want to prick you up like pepper. They're only after your money – d'you think they'd roll with you if you were a button-maker?
AXEL	I'm prepared to pay for my pleasures – alas, we men are not romantics, ma'am. Perhaps a closer contact with the world makes us less susceptible than the ladies to the lures of the imagination.
MOTHER	He'd have my fantasies off me now. I'd trade them, for a life.
AXEL	Your Majesty's life is the envy of most women.
MOTHER	Where does that put them? What have you ever done for the women of this country?
AXEL	I have the satisfaction of seeing this nation immeasurably stronger than when I took up the reins of office thirty years ago.
MOTHER	We've been at *WAR* thirty years!

AXEL	The voice of Sweden speaks to the world –
MOTHER	Never mind the voice, what about the eggs, where are the eggs?
AXEL	You have never understood the nature of war economy.
MOTHER	And when should I have learned that – I was pregnant for fifteen years.
AXEL	Precisely.
MOTHER	The women of this country don't need to understand theory. They're too busy keeping their families alive against the day you expose them to the sword.
AXEL	You spit on the shield that defends you.
MOTHER	You? Defend *US*?
AXEL	Who else?
MOTHER	The Queen! My daughter! Who's taking us out of this war? Not you!
CHRISTINA	*Thrusts back the curtains.*
CHRISTINA	Shut up, or I'll throw you both in the bloody clink. (To AXEL) What do you want?
AXEL	I've delayed council as long as possible. They insist on decision.
CHRISTINA	I will sign no edict that bans the mass – Goddamit, man, the Catholic countries are our major allies.
AXEL	That is foreign affairs. Matters of dogma touch on internal security. To allow mass to be celebrated is to increase nests of spies from one end of the country to the other.
CHRISTINA	But we can't break the law .. as ambassador, the man's on his own territory.
AXEL	It sets a precedent.

CHRISTINA   By God, is a man not to be allowed the thoughts in his head? Do you want a nation of dissemblers? What does it matter if we listen to dog latin or mournful sermons? No religion can be put to the proof.

AXEL   *(barks)* What?

CHRISTINA   I merely point out that the picture is relevant to the point of view. A matter of perspective.

AXEL   I am aware of Your Majesty's recent attachment to modern painting. May I ask that these extreme views be confined to the Royal quarters?

CHRISTINA   Oh, don't be a fool.

MOTHER   It's time they got a slap in the face. When are they going to vote my pension?

Pause.

AXEL   I must ask you to reconsider. There is a good deal of .. restlessness since we ended the war.

CHRISTINA *gives him a sharp look. Pause.*

            The nobles are speaking for a fresh campaign.
CHRISTINA   And I wonder who gardened that notion.

Pause.

CHRISTINA   I will not have our Catholic allies disaffected. There will be no more adventures .. campaigns.

Silence. A prolonged battle of wills.

            On the matter of my marriage ..

MOTHER	My love?
AXEL	On the matter of Your Majesty's marriage, the demand for decision becomes insistent. As Your Majesty well knows.
CHRISTINA	*(Pause)* Why all the fuss? They know I'll marry Karl.
MOTHER	Oh my love, at last! A wedding at last! We must begin preparations for the ceremony at once.
AXEL	If it could be annnounced on a formal basis.
CHRISTINA	Very well. If you insist.

He kisses her hand, to her surprise. The QUEEN MOTHER *promptly offers her hand, which is kissed.*

	And tell them to tear up their edict. You'd better send him in. The French ambassador.
MOTHER	He's a doctor, my love. Consult him.
AXEL	He is also a Catholic. I must ask Your Majesties to maintain reserve.

He bows and goes, triumphant. CHRISTINA *and her* MOTHER *make vile faces at his back, united for once.*

MOTHER   A wedding!

She embraces CHRISTINA *and kisses her.* CHRISTINA *flinches at the unexpected embrace, and extricates herself clumsily. To evade her mother she climbs back into bed, disturbing the bedclothes, and revealing a lightly clad, pretty girl.*

MOTHER	I should have known better than to expect a moment's happiness from you. I suppose I must be grateful you haven't got a donkey in there.

She goes. CHRISTINA *cuddles the girl.* CHANUT, *the French ambassador, enters, clears his throat politely.*

CHRISTINA	By God, you were quick! Ain't there no-one to present you?
CHANUT	Your Majesty's betrothal is being announced. My felicitations.
CHRISTINA	Oh that. They haven't wasted much time. Meet my bedfellow.
CHANUT	Enchanté. Your Majesty's taste is poetic. I trust that you are feeling better.
CHRISTINA	And I trust you've the wit to see I'm not.
CHANUT	May I?

CHANUT *examines her discreetly and deftly.*

You feel sick .. bilious?

CHRISTINA *nods.*

It feels tender here?

She nods. He completes his examination.

CHANUT	A crisis of the liver. What have your doctors ordered?
CHRISTINA	Hot cream, spiced meat and brandy.
GIRL	Which Her Majesty, being unable to stomach, forces me to eat.
CHANUT	Then you, too, lady, will be in a heated state before long.

CHRISTINA *smiles, dismisses the* GIRL.

CHRISTINA   This business of the mass.
CHANUT   I deeply regret to have caused you embarrassment.
CHRISTINA   Discretion, Monsieur! What news of Paris, I hear I'm known as a rake.
CHANUT   And as an intellectual.
CHRISTINA   They flatter me. Mere restlessness. I've been tricked into this marriage, you know.
CHANUT   The thought is not pleasing to you?
CHRISTINA   My dear Chanut, the prospect of royal marriage is about as attractive as a forced march through mud.
CHANUT   Very graphic, ma'am.

They laugh.

CHRISTINA   How others adapt to it is beyond me.
CHANUT   Your Majesty is too perceptive.
CHRISTINA   Then you predicate the need for royal fools. Not that I haven't sought achievement. In the accident of my estate. Peace .. prosperity ... a shining light from the north. And as I reach for the pinnacle, they will push me off into the byre.
CHANUT   Surely there are .. options? The world is full of possibilities.
CHRISTINA   So poor Monsieur Descartes had it, before our cruel Swedish winter finished him off.
              You Catholics disturb me. You bring a sweet, warm air from the south. Possibilities, eh? Perhaps I should change my condition. After all, it is the meek who will inherit the earth, are we not told?

CHANUT   A queen may practise humility, Your Majesty
              is a witness to that fact.

CHRISTINA   Our practise, Monsieur Chanut, is power..
              humility mere hobby. Which we have no wish
              to extend to humiliation. You're a handsome
              man. No, if I must marry I must .. but I'm
              damned if I'll breed for them and be destroyed,
              like my mother. He'd make a fine King, you
              said? The Prince Karl.

CHANUT   A thousand pardons, Majesty. I meant, of
              course, King-Consort.

CHRISTINA   I'll proclaim him my heir, that should placate –
              oh, don't be alarmed, Karl won't threaten my
              position. Amazing as it may seem he has an
              affection for us.

CHANUT   Why amazing?

CHRISTINA   Come, don't tell me that a man of your wit and
              style isn't amused at the thought of little Karl
              and me.

CHANUT   I see that Your Majesty horribly under-rates
              herself.

CHRISTINA   And I see that you seek to flatter like the rest of
              them. Look at me, man.

CHANUT   You find your appearance wanting? Is there a
              woman who does not?

CHRISTINA   Then it is a general condition.

CHANUT   Madame?

CHRISTINA   We live on sufferance. To your desires. I find
              you a cruel sex.

CHANUT   Madam, a man is powerless. Where his body
              stands, there must he follow.

CHRISTINA   No man follows me. They follow symmetry,
              and all the thought in the world won't give me
              that. No, I'm damned if I'll breed for them. I

	pollute enough space as it is.
CHANUT	For which I prescribe two days of fasting, followed by a diet of fruit and vegetables.
CHRISTINA	What?
CHANUT	Not an immediate cure. Chronic Puritan conscience tends to persist but we can make a start.
CHRISTINA	Fast, for two days?
CHANUT	Three would be better but Your Majesty is a beginner.
CHRISTINA	Three it shall be then.
CHANUT	With respect, ma'am, I prescribe two. We must try to secede from the stoic.
CHRISTINA	By God! We agree so well we shall be enemies in no time! Vegetables? Hardly a diet for a Queen.
CHANUT	Ah, but this is for the woman – forgive me, I spoke without thinking.
CHRISTINA	Oh I don't think you'd do that. You'd better be as good as the promise in those dark eyes. Good, I can't wait to start. *(She strokes his cheek, then goes quickly without ceremony)*

CHANUT'S SECRETARY *appears, to take dictation.*

CHANUT	You will be pleased to hear that we maintain a most cordial climate with Snowdrop. Our personal relations are .. no .. erase that. Spiritually there is growth, but soil conditions remain poor and the outlook is bleak. However, I have to report a unique climatic possibility. Our flower now refers, albeit indirectly, to transplantation. In which case there is the possible replacement of

Snowdrop by Cabbage. Is this in our interest? Underline that please. I request instruction with urgency ... we remain etc., etc.   P.S. We now hold mass openly. Attendance this morning, 24, including two German converts and an elderly Swede. No question about it – she's coming our way.

SECRETARY   Very puzzling, sir.

CHANUT   Puzzling? It's downright dangerous. You'd better keep a valise packed. We may need to make a sudden journey.

SECRETARY   Sir?

CHANUT   If there's one thing Protestants enjoy as much as good Catholics, dear boy, it's a scapegoat. I wonder if this is the right job for you. *(An arm about the young man's shoulder as they leave)*

SECRETARY   I beg your pardon, Uncle?

SCENE FIVE

Impasse

A TABLE, *formal.* AXEL *enters, followed by* KARL, *the* DUKE, *an older man, and* COPLEMAN, *a merchant.* CHRISTINA *follows on their heels.*

CHRISTINA   Good morning!

They sit.

Let me see the agenda. Good. We'll reverse the order. Propose the last motion.

Silence.

AXEL	Very well. Proposed.
CHRISTINA	Copleman?
COPLEMAN	Seconded, ma'am. *(The* DUKE *glares at him)*
CHRISTINA	On the matter of the succession, are we ready to ratify? The matter lies on the table.

Silence.

DUKE	The succession of His Highness, the Prince Karl, in advance of the royal nuptials, could hardly be agreeable to the Swedish people.
CHRISTINA	Oh? And since when have they been asked? *(Slight pause)* The object is to secure succession in case of accident. Suppose I break me neck on the hunting field? Copleman, you speak for the merchants.
COPLEMAN	It is our humble opinion that His Royal Highness, Prince Karl, would be more than worthy to .. ah .. reign over Sweden, should that unhappy eventuality arise.
CHRISTINA	Good. Good, then that settles it. I have the casting vote.
AXEL	No.

Silence.

CHRISTINA	Why?
AXEL	The vote is premature.

Silence.

DUKE	There are stringent days ahead. Now that we've chosen to end the war. His Royal

	Highness might well face a shortage of funds.
CHRISTINA	They don't trust you Karl. Or they think I'm a fool. You've got the betrothal, what more do you want?
AXEL	The marriage.
DUKE	We need the marriage.
CHRISTINA	It's too late for the summer.
AXEL	The autumn, then.
CHRISTINA	We're here to ratify the succession, *NOT* the date of a wedding. This matter is on the table and I will have it resolved.

Silence.

Very well, adjourn the council.

She turns away. The DUKE *and* COPLEMAN *bow and leave.*

AXEL	What do you think you're doing?
CHRISTINA	You know very well what I'm doing.
AXEL	If we ratify the succession will you agree to the autumn?
CHRISTINA	What wouldn't you do to have me staked down .. tried Chanut's diet yet, Karl?
KARL	Anything to please, cousin.
CHRISTINA	I doubt if you'd take to it. *(She waves, dismissing him, he goes)*
AXEL	I don't deny that I shall be relieved. The beauties of both sexes that you see fit to keep about you are costing the privy purse a fortune.
CHRISTINA	Oh come, a few wild oats, surely?
AXEL	So far as I'm concerned, once there's an heir, you can do as you please.

CHRISTINA, I see. Tell me, how many royal confinements do you require before I'm allowed to fornicate? To secure this throne, give or take a miscarriage or so, will take the next twenty years of my life. If it doesn't put me under the ground.

AXEL   The same for all women.

CHRISTINA All the more reason to stay chaste.

AXEL   Have you been listening to that damned Catholic? Hang him about your neck much longer, you'll have the whole nobility affected. Resign yourself. They will not have the succession without the marriage. And if you continue to prate about choice, freedom, and all the other fashionable rubbish you'll have the church at your throat and I shan't answer for your future, your throne or your personal safety. Have I made myself clear?

CHRISTINA *(loud)* Don't bully me! I grew up with it. Your stinking sweat, bellowing in my ears for as long as I can remember.

AXEL   Fulfilling my duty.

CHRISTINA Why didn't you leave me in the parlour with the rest of the women, it's what you want!

AXEL   Not at all. Your unique position demands both the manly qualities of a king, and the fecundity of a woman.

CHRISTINA Well you can't *have* both.

AXEL   Why not? For twenty years I've prepared you for it.

CHRISTINA And how? By making a man of me. A man, despising women – just like you. You've had your joke, you and nature between you.

AXEL   I have performed a duty to your father, and to
                Sweden.
CHRISTINA   You've never even liked me.
AXEL   You have more power, more land than any
                king before you. Thanks to me.
CHRISTINA   And you've lived! You've had a full life!
                Soldier, courtier, lover .... you even allowed
                your own daughters to marry where their
                desires led them. You've been a fond father.
AXEL   I hope so.
CHRISTINA   You denied me all of it. I don't even engage
                your lubricity. I must be unique in Sweden for
                that.
AXEL   Madam, have I your permission to withdraw?
CHRISTINA   No. You never even liked me.

                I will be more discreet, with the Frenchman.
                We'll create a new bishop, that should placate
                the Church.

AXEL   Very good. *(Bows)*
CHRISTINA   But .. *(He pauses)* ... you will respect me.
AXEL   Madam?
CHRISTINA   You will respect the man you've created.
AXEL   In what way?
CHRISTINA   Secure the succession. You may as well know,
                I am not of a mind to marry.
AXEL   What? These perverse practices –
CHRISTINA   Nothing to do with my habits.
AXEL   Another suitor then! A blacksmith if you will
                but you must choose! Goddamit, woman, you
                seek to lay the blame at my door – did I make
                the world? You are a woman, it's your destiny
                to marry.

CHRISTINA   No! Haven't you humiliated me enough ... no!
Do you think I haven't been tempted, with half
Europe willing to close its eyes and bed me?
No.

You've done your job too well. I love men!
Their company, their talk ... the smell of a
man's sweat in the saddle! I love them in the
bone ... in the flesh ... the wildness ... the pricky
insolence. The truth that is in a man takes him
where his flesh decides. The flesh chooses! Do
you think I'm going to pollute that, the only
truth I know?'

I will not rape a man. Nor will I be the woman
for you to despise. Between the two you have
put me off. I've dreamed of murdering you for
it.

Pause.

AXEL   What is to be done?
CHRISTINA   Secure the succession. Don't be a fool, man.
Do it for your own sake.

He looks at her for a long moment, turns and goes.

CHRISTINA   By God, I've frightened him. Hah! The Queen
of Sweden, a Catholic convert ... but no doubt
without a country.

EBBA *enters.*

(cool) Hullo, Belle, what can we do for you?

EBBA   You've been so busy since we returned from
              Paris. I wanted to thank you for paying our
              debts.
CHRISTINA   Magnus has his army appointment.
EBBA   I came to see you. I'd like to think we were still
              friends.
CHRISTINA   You're as beautiful as ever.
EBBA   It slips away. The shine goes.
CHRISTINA   What are you trying to do, console me?
EBBA   I hear you don't need it.
CHRISTINA   Ah, the witty Chanut! How was Paris?
EBBA   Everything we dreamed of .. poetic,
              astringent, full of life and charm. And the
              women .. amazing!
CHRISTINA   The women?
EBBA   They call them blue-stockings – it's a fashion,
              they wear them. Such independence – they
              read, write, publish ... some of the blue-
              stockings are even refusing to marry!
CHRISTINA   What?!
EBBA   They revere you, Pixie, they couldn't hear
              enough of you.
CHRISTINA   Indeed? Come here .. I've missed you.

She pulls EBBA *to her. And lets go at once.*

CHRISTINA   Get out. I will not have pregnant cows under
              my roof. Let me look at you. Ugh, how could
              you?
EBBA   Pixie, it is natural.
CHRISTINA   So's plague.
EBBA   *(quietly)* What's the matter?
CHRISTINA   Nothing.
EBBA   Tell me.

CHRISTINA	Can you feel it, does it move?
EBBA	Oh yes .. it lives.
CHRISTINA	I may be going to Rome.
EBBA	Rome?
CHRISTINA	To see the Holy Father.
EBBA	Christina, you can't! You mustn't even think of it!
CHRISTINA	I've been toying with Catholicism .. the new scepticism ... at least it's arguable. I find no answers in this cauldron of ice.
EBBA	You will find the Catholics less accommodating than you think. Christina these are dangerous thoughts, they attack your position.
CHRISTINA	Oh don't worry. If I convert they will throw me out. There is another reason. I don't intend to marry.
EBBA	Not marry? Why not?
CHRISTINA	Your trouble, my girl, is that you're too fond of the men.
EBBA	You like them too, now don't deny it, Pixie.
CHRISTINA	Yes but they don't like me ... so I'm out of it. I might as well be a free rover. Let somebody else breed the tribe. I choose not to. Anyway, what are you worried about, you've got what's in your belly. Oh, what do you want me to say – that you look wonderful, that your skin glows like a pearl – *(approaches* EBBA) are you in milk?
EBBA	No. That comes later.
CHRISTINA	Well, God be with you. I'm sure you'll do well.

EBBA *bows and goes.*

That's his son you've got ... or his daughter!

And there'll be more, a brood of beauties like the lilies of the field, striding across their lives ...

She could be dead by Michaelmas.

Rome.

CHANUT *enters.*

CHANUT	Madame, I must speak with you!
CHRISTINA	You've heard.
CHANUT	You cannot be serious. You will ruin both of us. Please, I beg you to consider .. please! *(on his knees).*
CHRISTINA	Not so unattainable now.
CHANUT	*(bewildered)* But what have you not had from me? And all our talk .. did you not understand the nature of it? The conversion of Sweden ... the bringing of light and life to the north – you agreed! With you as our ally, the whole of Europe to be embraced in the Catholic cloak!
CHRISTINA	A fine design.
CHANUT	But without your throne, what are you?
CHRISTINA	What indeed?
CHANUT	Are you mad? Have you not understood?
CHRISTINA	My poor man. Having to close your eyes and bed me. And all for nought.
CHANUT	Not so, I swear not so. But this is personal. I beg of you to listen, these matters are vital!

CHRISTINA *makes to go. He follows.*

CHANUT	You *MUST* marry Karl!

Abdication

CHRISTINA'S *silver throne is set.*

AXEL *enters, with cane. He looks older, walks with a limp, his face slightly twisted, as though he has had a stroke.*

KARL *enters.* AXEL *crosses to* KARL, *bows.*

KARL	There is not a foot of space in the square. People are jammed against the cathedral doors.
AXEL	Trouble?
KARL	None. They are silent, utterly silent. Ah, Bishop. *(The* BISHOP *approaches and bows to him)*
BISHOP	A grievous day, Sire.
KARL	Yes ... yes, indeed. We must all hope, even at this late stage ... is that not the case, Chancellor?

AXEL *turns away grimly.*

EBBA *enters, supporting the* QUEEN MOTHER.

MOTHER	You see? They want the Queen, they'll have no-one else! *(to* KARL) Traitor! Are they going to cut us to pieces?
BISHOP	Most gracious Majesty ..
MOTHER	Ah, my Lord Bishop. Tell them all to go home, we can't have this sort of thing. *(Vicious, of* AXEL) He's no good, what has he done? Make her do as she's told! *(to* EBBA) Why

can't she be like you, you mother's got three
sons, is that fair .. I ask, is that fair?

EBBA   Please, madam, come away.

MAGNUS *enters, bows to the* QUEEN MOTHER, *crosses to*
KARL, *confers in a whisper.*

MOTHER   What is it, has she changed her mind ... there
you are. I told you, she's changed her mind!
Abdication! What nonsense! There's no
ceremony, no dress for such an occasion ....
give up, Karl! Traitor!

EBBA   Madam, you distress yourself.

MOTHER   *(rationally)* Don't worry, my dear. She isn't
coming.

The MUSIC *starts.* CHRISTINA *appears quietly. She wears
white, as for a wedding, the crown on her head. As she appears
the music comes to an end.*

MOTHER   Look at her! She thinks it's a wedding, she
thinks it's a wedding, she thinks it's a wedding!

She shrieks with hysterical laughter.

CHRISTINA *takes her position.*

KARL   There is still time.

CHRISTINA   My Lord Chancellor?

AXEL *looks at her, then nods to* BISHOP. *A drumroll.
Plainsong. The* BISHOP *moves forward. He can't find his
place in the prayer book, sniffs, wipes his nose with a white
handkerchief.*

Oh, get on with it, man.

The BISHOP *mumbles prayers in a cracked wail. A murmur of* '*amen*'. *Plainsong.*

Hiatus. No-one knows what to do next. CHRISTINA *looks about the assembly, then to the* BISHOP.

CHRISTINA	Bishop, I think you must now take the crown from my head.
MOTHER	Not at all, not at all.
KARL	Christina please! Stay on any terms!
CHRISTINA	Bishop ...

The BISHOP *approaches, lifts his hands over her head, then*

BISHOP	I cannot do it, Majesty. If it were to cost me my head I could not – *(he gives way)*
CHRISTINA	But you must.

He stands before her, head bowed.

EBBA	No!
KARL	Please!
MAGNUS	Don't go, ma'am!
EBBA	Please..
KARL	Christina, there is still time. Think .. think ..
MOTHER	She mustn't .. don't let her .. don't let her ...
EBBA	Sweden begs you..

CHRISTINA *gives her a long look.*

CHRISTINA	My Lord Chancellor, will you do it?
AXEL	There is still time. Nothing is irreversible.
CHRISTINA	Come, take your crown. After all, it is fitting –

you've been its guardian all your life.
Is it too much to ask?

AXEL   You know my heart.

CHRISTINA   Don't tell me I've broken your heart – I never had it. Very well. Retire with honour and breed your fine horses. Karl .. Karl, you must do it.

KARL   Not I, Christina.

MOTHER   Make her stay, Karl, she'll listen to you, she likes you – take Karl, marry Karl ... he'll do!

Pause.

CHRISTINA   Will you take it from me?

KARL shakes his head.

Karl .. take the crown from me.
I order you.
Must it fall to the ground?

She takes off the crown, holds it out, as though to drop it. KARL takes the crown from her. The Queen Mother gives way in Magnus's arms.

(*to* KARL) I've treated you badly. But it wouldn't have done, you know.

She kisses KARL on the cheek. He bows, thrusts the crown into MAGNUS' hands and leaves. MAGNUS bows briefly to CHRISTINA and follows his new master eagerly.

The BISHOP bows low and leaves. CHRISTINA crosses to EBBA, who is supporting the QUEEN MOTHER. The QUEEN MOTHER grasps CHRISTINA and clings to her fiercely.

CHRISTINA It's all right, it's all right, it's all right.

She unpins a large sapphire and diamond brooch, pins it to her mother's breast.

MOTHER   But it's your best one! Look .. look, she's given me her best one!

EBBA begins to lead the QUEEN MOTHER away. The QUEEN MOTHER exits as CHRISTINA detains EBBA by the sleeve. She kisses EBBA.

CHRISTINA Don't forget me.

EBBA goes.

CHRISTINA and AXEL are left. She makes a slight move towards him but he turns away. At a distance he turns back and they regard each other for a long moment. He goes.

CHRISTINA stands. Then, in a whirl of movement, she rips off her dress to reveal riding clothes underneath, and boots. She throws the dress across the space onto the throne, whirls round, her arms out in ecstasy, and leaves at the run.

SCENE ONE

Tea With A Visitor

A sunlit room. The staging is not naturalistic, but there is a civilised quality, in contrast to the brutal surroundings in Act One. Some upholstery, flowers, and decoration in blue and yellow.

The MARQUISE *enters. She is plumpish, soft-skinned, soft-voiced. Her grey gown is trimmed with white, simply cut, but ferociously elegant and well-fitting. She is followed by her friend, Catherine de Rohant, younger, more severely dressed. She carries a book.*

Behind them comes a footman carrying a large tray set with wine and cakes.

MARQUISE   Here. No – there.

The FOOTMAN *sets down the tray.*

CATHERINE Splendid. And flowers!
MARQUISE   I thought cakes with the claret – I believe she
                     has a sweet tooth.
CATHERINE The Queen of Sweden. Our most important
                     coup.
MARQUISE   Yes. Here she will see how we live .. our
                     work .. the looms .. the farm ....
CATHERINE And all without men.

A bell, off.

MARQUISE   She is here! *(She nods to the* FOOTMAN, *who exits)*

The women compose themselves to receive CHRISTINA. *The* FOOTMAN *enters, and* CHRISTINA *pushes in behind him, nervous and eager. She wears battered riding clothes, over which she has draped a skirt in honour of the visit. She doffs her plumed hat in greeting.*

The two women curtsey, deeply and impeccably.

CHRISTINA   Oh no ceremony ladies, please .. we left all that in Sweden. Madame la Marquise?

She thrusts out a hand which misses the MARQUISE *who is curtseying again.*

MARQUISE   May I present Madame de Rohant?

CHRISTINA *shakes her hand, then sits.*

CHRISTINA   Lovely room, I like the blue and yellow .. Swedish colours you know.
MARQUISE   Yes, Majesty.
CHRISTINA   What? Oh, you mean you did it for me? Good .. very nice. *(to* CATHERINE) What did you say your name was?
CATHERINE   Catherine de Rohant, ma'am.
CHRISTINA   I've read your thoughts on the condition of women!
CATHERINE   Madame, your name rings through Europe.
MARQUISE   The Queen of Sweden declines to marry.

CHRISTINA *grins, cramming her face with cakes.*

CATHERINE   To refuse to procreate, even at the cost of a throne!

CHRISTINA   Oh, I wasn't kicked out, if that's what they're saying – no, no – decision was mine!

CATHERINE You have asserted the freedom of all women!

MARQUISE   Meeting you, Majesty, is the high point of our lives!

CHRISTINA   Me too ... though I must say, I'm very disappointed ... *(she sits back, wiping her hands in her skirts)* I mean ... where are they?

The women are mystified and alarmed .. what can have gone wrong? CHRISTINA swoops, jerking up the MARQUISE'S skirts. The Marquise jumps to her feet with a shriek of alarm.

CHRISTINA   The stockings .. the blue stockings! Shan't believe a word of it without the blue stockings!

She laughs uproariously, and they join in, realising that it is a 'joke'.

MARQUISE   *(waits for CHRISTINA to contain her merriment)* Highness, a toast.

She gestures to the FOOTMAN, who pours drinks. CHRISTINA knocks hers straight back, so the MARQUISE takes over, re-pours, the FOOTMAN takes a glass to CATHERINE.

A toast, Majesty. What shall we drink to?

CATHERINE Why, to women!

They murmur, and drink. Hiatus. The Frenchwomen wait for CHRISTINA to speak first.

CHRISTINA   *(pause)* You married?

CATHERINE My husband and I are separated, ma'am.

CHRISTINA Any children?

CATHERINE Two boys. They are away at school.

CHRISTINA How old?

CATHERINE Two and four.

CHRISTINA Seems a bit young.

MARQUISE *(soft)* Madame de Rohant is much concerned with her writing.

CHRISTINA What about you, your husband's dead, I believe.

MARQUISE I am, happily, freed from that subjection, ma'am.

CHRISTINA Didn't you like it?

MARQUISE My purpose was to provide heirs for my husband's title and property. Women, Majesty, are no more than fields for growing corn.

CHRISTINA By God, you're right. What about sex though, don't you miss it?

MARQUISE As Your Majesty well knows, men have not the exclusive rights to our bodies.

CHRISTINA Oh you mean you're together? Jolly good.

CATHERINE To submit to men is treachery to our cause. The enemy must be attacked, does Your Majesty not agree?

CHRISTINA *(at the drink)* To be honest, the word enemy chills my liver after thirty years at war. I see your point .. the need to be extreme. You ain't afraid of being laughed at?

CATHERINE On the contrary, we are well aware that we are considered highly ridiculous .. not the least by other women, who call us traitors to our sex.

MARQUISE And who will be the first to exploit the benefits we achieve on their behalf.

CATHERINE We are on the move, Majesty. In the end, all

slaves rebel.

CHRISTINA I'm sure you're right, though to tell the truth I've never much enjoyed the company of women, you can't get any sense out of them. *(Pause, she realises she has put her foot in it)*

MARQUISE Madame, is that surprising?

CHRISTINA No .. yes, see what you mean. Stuck in the kitchen, that sort of thing – no, not fair.

CATHERINE Rumour has it, Majesty, that you have converted.

CHRISTINA Who told you? Well, since we're among friends – yes, I'm on my way to Rome! I mean to be at the centre of things .. to expand, with Messer Copernicus, Signor Galileo .. devote myself to research at the feet of the Holy Father.

CATHERINE The Pope, Majesty, is a man.

MARQUISE Your Majesty's conversion is devout?

CHRISTINA Lord, no, I'm a sceptic.

The FOOTMAN *enters with a letter.*

MARQUISE I gave strict instructions that we were not to be disturbed. *(The* FOOTMAN *whispers in her ear)* Forgive me, Majesty, a crisis it seems.

She reads the letter, hands it to CATHERINE.

CHRISTINA Bad news?

MARQUISE My father. He is failing. The heart.

CHRISTINA We must be deprived of your company. So sad.

CATHERINE There is no question of your going. Put it to the test. Would such a visit further our cause, or impede it? I am certain of the answer.

MARQUISE There *is* pneumonia in the lungs.

CATHERINE Then I trust he has good nurses.
MARQUISE I will write a letter.

She does so.

CATHERINE You find us harsh.
CHRISTINA Why yes .. yes, a little.

The MARQUISE *gives the letter to the* FOOTMAN, *who goes.*

CHRISTINA You hate all men?
CATHERINE It is necessary.
CHRISTINA I begin to feel like an impostor.
CATHERINE You are an inspiration to us all. You have shown us the way!
CHRISTINA But I only pushed off because I couldn't stand it. I wanted to live!
CATHERINE Precisely! Why shouldn't we demand the same freedoms as men – more, since the breeding of children confines us more!
MARQUISE With you at our side, ma'am, there is nothing we cannot accomplish.
CHRISTINA I honour your courage.
CATHERINE We may rely on your true support?
CHRISTINA I will write to you – from Rome. By the way, my French ambassador is in Paris. He's a fine doctor, I recommend him. *(They curtsey and she goes)*
CATHERINE What do you think?
MARQUISE I think she's slipped us. It was the business of my father.
CATHERINE She's naive. And a moralist.
MARQUISE Yes. All this fervour for the Pope.

CATHERINE   The nobility of Rome will soon tire of an ex-
            Queen at table, then where will she be? We
            recruit them all as their breasts fall.
MARQUISE   How harsh you are. The Queen of Sweden is
            an important ally.
CATHERINE   Then we'll pursue her.
MARQUISE   Pity she's so little to look at.
CATHERINE   Yes. Whatever was she wearing?

SCENE TWO

Papa

The Vatican. The CARDINALS *and* CHRISTINA, *apart,
wait for the* POPE. *The* POPE *enters, a handsome man in the
prime of life.*

POPE   Our dear daughter.

CHRISTINA *rushes at him, tries to throw her arms about his
neck, a* CARDINAL *intervenes. She smothers the* POPE'S
hand with kisses.

POPE   Beloved daughter. Welcome to Rome. We are
            beside ourself, our joy is without bounds.
CHRISTINA   Oh Papa, my lovely Papa! We've waited so
            long!
POPE   No tears, my daughter.
CHRISTINA   They're tears of joy, to see your face at last! So
            handsome! Much better than the pictures – the
            coins are a slander on that nose, that profile!
POPE   You are too loving. We accept your love. We
            welcome such a loving heart to our bosom.

CHRISTINA   *(Draws a chair close)* We've been so hungry for this moment – what? What's the matter with the man?

The POPE *lifts a benevolent hand and the* CARDINAL *draws back.*

CHRISTINA   I'm hungry for food .. for truth .. philosophy. We long for talk.

POPE   A garden has been prepared for you. Fine walks, and much shade. The Palace is not so large, but very fine. You will like the views.

CHRISTINA   Where we'll sit together and talk about the meaning of meaning .. of life, light, and the new astronomy – I can't wait, Pope! We flew across Europe – well, with the odd dalliance, you won't begrudge me that after years of toil, very good for the bowels, I recommend it.

The CARDINALS *hiss displeasure.*

POPE   *(with a sweet smile)* We have heard of your adventures, daughter. It has come to our attention.

CHRISTINA   Oh. I've been a real rogue, whored my way across Europe! For which I hope you'll hear my confession – I've a tale or two to relate, I can tell you.

POPE   Confession connotes repentance.

CHRISTINA   Oh I don't repent. Best time I ever had in my life .. that's something we're going to have to put right in your religion. Celibacy's no good – not in the Bible, you know. Think again ..˙no need to cut it off, Pope!

The CARDINALS *react with shock. The* POPE *waves them back.*

> The chastity of Jesus – no more than an assumption ... and to copy it an arrogant act, since God has fashioned us as coupling creatures. Deny the design of creation? Devilish work, Pope. At least, that's my opinion.

POPE   There is much to be achieved here. Humility, daughter. We commend your thoughts to loving humility.

Light change. The CARDINALS *go. The* POPE *and* CHRISTINA *with her arms round her knees.*

POPE   Christina, we are not mere animals, subject to season, to blind instinct. God has given us consciousness. To treat other people as a means to an end is both to deny justice, and the inner life. In matters of the sensual, the carnal, there is always another person to be considered, the possibility of exploitation. *(Slight pause)* We come to the question of self-disgust.

CHRISTINA   To enjoy a meal together .. is that disgusting? To sing in unison? Where's the fault in it?

POPE   This is a false innocence.

CHRISTINA   You mean I buy my loves? There's a reason in that.

POPE   My daughter, what reason can you give me?

CHRISTINA   My face.

Light change. CHRISTINA *and the* POPE, *now sitting further apart.*

POPE   We are disturbed. We would be reassured that
            Your Majesty's decision to abdicate was not,
            as rumour persists, taken for reasons of
            defiance.

CHRISTINA   Rumours. What rumours now?

POPE   That you reject the marriage bed. That you
            refuse to procreate.

CHRISTINA   Is that so bad? Where does it put you? Sorry,
            Pope, freewill .. I concede.

POPE   You are a woman, with a sacred destiny.
            Without procreation, mutual love, and loving
            care, society cannot hold.

CHRISTINA   No copulation without a swelled belly or we're
            in sin, is that it?

POPE   *(shakes his head)* Marriage is for procreation,
            for the orientation of desire, and thus for
            harmonious conjugal life.

CHRISTINA   Oh, we're allowed a little fun in the marriage
            bed? Hah .. take my mother. Eighteen
            pregnancies, stillbirths, premature drop .. dead
            infants in the churchyard, unnamed corpses,
            flesh of her flesh, torn, cut out .. you should see
            that woman's quarters, she can neither sit nor
            stand without pain. And don't tell me she's
            blessed to suffer in the name of the Lord, the
            woman's banal. She's banal because of it.

POPE   Alas, the need for an heir.

CHRISTINA   So you would sanction the exploitation of the
            female? What's wrong with intervention, I see
            you avail yourself of physic.

POPE   Thank you for your good wishes and gifts
            during my fever.

CHRISTINA   It's still the quinine that's put you on your feet.
            Intervention, Pope. Intervention.

POPE   We have heard of your views on the bearing of children. If parenthood is excluded from marriage, why then the character of the relation is utterly diminished.

CHRISTINA   What's wrong with pleasure? *(Pause)* What about sexual need?

POPE   We employ the urge for natural purposes, for which it was created. Where it threatens to degrade, to corrupt, we abjure, we employ continence.

CHRISTINA   Pope, you ignore nature!

POPE   Nature cannot be conquered by violating its laws! We know of these practices! Of the murder of the child in the womb! We are in a state of grief. These are dreadful acts – your influence becomes baleful.

CHRISTINA   But women are in need!

POPE   Woman is creation! Would you turn her into an assassin? What of the child, in the womb? What of its sacred life?

CHRISTINA   And what of a woman's flow? A child a month, deceased. And a man's ejaculation? Whole armies, whole populations denied breath. Nature is wasteful, Pope. We must look to ourselves.

POPE   This comes near blasphemy.

CHRISTINA   I don't intend to defy, nor to reject. But you say that you understand .. that your pastoral gives you knowledge, even at second-hand. You do not know. You abstract yourselves. You use yourselves up in dealing with your frustrations, with the ruination of your body selves. And you would condemn those of us who live in the world. You speak of love, and you would destroy us.

You're a smart, careful man, and you live by a complexity of rule from a wide gathering, and it gives you conviction. But where are you in your nakedness?

I will quieten down my private life .. not to embarrass you under your walls. But I cannot close my mouth. I seek guidance. But by brotherly, sisterly discourse. I'm on the move, you see. *(The* POPE *rises)* Don't disaffect me.

POPE   We are not angry. My daughter, if you do not feel yourself drawn to the true God, through His medium, the Church, to the command to love .. to charity .. why then ... I pray for your soul. *(He makes the sign of the cross on her forehead)* Be at peace.

He goes.

CHRISTINA   *(bitter)* The command to love? And what of the command to *BE* loved .. who can command that?

You bloody, handsome, arrogant man!

What a charmer. What a waste! And what a devil.

We won't deny the body. Never mind self-mutilating priests .. *(presses her hands to her body)* you shall be placated .. you shall be

loved! If not for desire then for my purse –
come on, man .. out of the shadows .. let's take
a look at you.

MONALDESCHO *moves forward.*

MONALDESCHO Madonna ... ah, bellissima!

CHRISTINA Do you know who I am?

MONALDESCHO I only know, mysterious stranger, that
my life is forever changed. Whoever you
are, wherever you are, I beg to follow
and serve you for the rest of your days ...
may they be as beautiful as your smile.

CHRISTINA *laughs heartily. Encouraged,*
MONALDESCHO *pursues her.*

MONALDESCHO If fortune is cruel .. if circumstance does
not permit .. why then I shall sit at your
gate, living for the moment when you
pass .. for your shadow .. for the print of
your heel on the grass .. *(He kisses her
foot, she kicks him away genially)*

CHRISTINA Get away, you must know who I am.

MONALDESCHO Only that you are a wild, eager fawn .. a
hare, soft, panting ... *(into her ear)*

CHRISTINA What's your name?

MONALDESCHO *(deep bow)* I am, cara madonna, your
devoted and humble servant, the
Marchese di Monaldescho. But we
forget rank, adorable stranger – I spit on
convention.

CHRISTINA You know very well I'm the Queen of Sweden.

MONALDESCHO A Queen? But I would not dare –

CHRISTINA Oh, I think you would.

MONALDESCHO *(pause)* I am dismissed?

CHRISTINA Not necessarily. Only don't presume too far for your pretty face.

MONALDESCHO But I love you.

CHRISTINA *(harsh)* What?

MONALDESCHO You are a Queen!

CHRISTINA Oh, I like it! Honest trade! In a country where nepotism is virtue and a bribe common sense – at least there's human warmth in it. *(She moves away)*

MONALDESCHO *(Uncertain)* Madonna?

CHRISTINA *(objective)* What use are you to me? What can you do?

MONALDESCHO I ask only to serve.

CHRISTINA Hah.

MONALDESCHO Whatever you desire is yours! I will provide. You shall be Queen of Rome – Queen of the world!

CHRISTINA I want the best.

MONALDESCHO Already yours.

CHRISTINA The best painters, the best sculptors, the best dancers ...

MONALDESCHO *(escorting her off)* But of course.

CHRISTINA What did you say your name was?

SCENE THREE

Forever Roma

CHRISTINA *and* MONALDESCHO, *lying together, chatting quietly.*

MONALDESCHO I'm not ambitious. No more than the next man. All I ask is some responsibility .. a piece of land to leave my children.

CHRISTINA Instead of which, you find yourself a lackey.

MONALDESCHO Ah, but to a Queen.

CHRISTINA Don't tell me you're a romantic.

MONALDESCHO I take what the world offers and count myself lucky that I please. You're not complaining, are you?

CHRISTINA No. Though I wish there could be more honest connection between us.

MONALDESCHO Who's the romantic now? There's limitation in all things. To be Alexander was to die young .. and the Virgin was probably plain.

CHRISTINA *(laughs)* What can I give you to make you happy?

MONALDESCHO Why should you please me?

CHRISTINA Why indeed .. I hold the purse. A logical man.

MONALDESCHO I have to be, I have dependants.

CHRISTINA Yes, we have discovered the wife and children. We are so pleased when you tell us the truth.

MONALDESCHO As often as I can, that's common sense.

CHRISTINA How real you are. A survivor. You may even survive me.

MONALDESCHO Do I need to?

CHRISTINA Of course not. Have you ordered the centrepiece for the dinner table?

MONALDESCHO Not yet.

CHRISTINA Good. I want the Descent from the Cross. In pink sugar.

A New Game

CHRISTINA *on stage.*

CHRISTINA *(calls, in a rage)* Monaldescho!

MONALDESCHO *(off)* Yes? *(He enters, eating, pulling on his jacket)* Yes?

CHRISTINA Mind your manners.

MONALDESCHO I couldn't come any faster, what do you want?

CHRISTINA Bend your bloody leg, that's what I want.

MONALDESCHO You're in a bad mood this morning.

CHRISTINA And you're getting too quick for your own good.

MONALDESCHO I have to be pretty smart to keep us out of the bankruptcy court.

CHRISTINA That's your affair, I pay you enough.

MONALDESCHO What's the matter with you, anyway?

CHRISTINA I'm bored!

MONALDESCHO There's a Cardinal here.

CHRISTINA Let him wait – I'm bored, I tell you! If something doesn't happen soon, I shall commit murder.

AZZOLINO *(at the entrance)* Perhaps Your Majesty needs a new direction.

CHRISTINA Who let you in?

AZZOLINO God. And the Pope, of course.

CHRISTINA *waves* MONALDESCHO off.

CHRISTINA What are you here for, to scold me again?

AZZOLINO No, my daughter. His Holiness sends warm greetings, and his love.

CHRISTINA He must want something. *(She sits, indicates for him to sit)*

AZZOLINO Your Majesty continues to be .. happy in Rome?

CHRISTINA You were listening. I'm bored. I was bred for work. It seems that without the whip one loses direction .. even my intuition deserts me. One becomes a sort of shifting fable. I've come to the conclusion that the world lacks meaning.

AZZOLINO Purpose and meaning are not objective facts. Value exists in ourselves, not in the world. Integration is decided by choice .. it is we who decide who we are.

CHRISTINA I knew who I was in Sweden – why not here?

AZZOLINO Alas, when we are thrown back on ourselves we perceive only that we do not exist.

CHRISTINA What sort of conundrum's that? *(Slight pause)* I exist. Something feels. Perhaps you can tell me why, having left that Lutheran prison in order to enjoy my life, it seems impossible that I should do so. Why must there be interpretation?

AZZOLINO It may be that you seek a cause.

CHRISTINA The cause of service is an impertinence which you know full well I've abandoned. Sweden was lucky I was poxed or vicious. At least here my influence is confined to empty ceremony. Which I might enjoy since I've taste enough for the frivolous if it were not for the fact that, having come to the conclusion that life is meaningless, I'm still invaded by the conviction that it ought not to be so.

AZZOLINO *(slight pause)* There is concern for the Kingdom of Naples. *(He sighs)* Alas, the

	people there cry out to be free.
CHRISTINA	What are you doing, offering me the Crown? You're a handsome man, Monsieur Cardinal.
AZZOLINO	Thank you, Majesty.
CHRISTINA	A handsome man, bearing gifts. I must be careful. Spain won't give up Naples, not without a fight. Oh, you want me for a fight? No, not even for your beautiful eyes.
AZZOLINO	Your statecraft is renowned.
CHRISTINA	Nor for your flattery, Cardinal. Tell me, are you chaste?
AZZOLINO	*(smiles)* I must ask Your Majesty to forebear.
CHRISTINA	No, no .. you must answer.
AZZOLINO	Madam, I cannot.
CHRISTINA	Suppose I order you to?
AZZOLINO	Such – discipline would be hard to resist.
CHRISTINA	Good, you're a naughty man. Naples eh?
AZZOLINO	A cause worthy of wit and intention .. the cause of freedom.
CHRISTINA	I doubt the Neapolitans will savour one foreign boot more than another.
AZZOLINO	Madam, they will greet you as a saviour.
CHRISTINA	But will they fight?
AZZOLINO	They are hot for revenge.
CHRISTINA	Hot, are they?
AZZOLINO	Perhaps Your Majesty would care to see papers?
CHRISTINA	*(peruses the papers)* Pity about your chastity. We've no need to do anything. Nothing directly carnal.
AZZOLINO	Alas, it is impossible.
CHRISTINA	Come, you're an Italian.
AZZOLINO	A poor emissary. On a failing mission, it seems.

CHRISTINA I wonder how I might be more .. compliant.

They regard each other.

We will consider your matter. With attention.

AZZOLINO There speaks the daughter of Gustavus Adolphus.

CHRISTINA My father? He's dead, man .. and so am I, I think.

AZZOLINO I do not believe it.

CHRISTINA Well, we will acquaint you of our purpose. Come tomorrow. The motives of the Holy Father –

AZZOLINO Are towards the alleviation of suffering. He knows your generous heart, and your respect for freedom.

CHRISTINA We'll talk again.

She kisses the ring. The CARDINAL *bows and goes.*

By God, they must want me out of Rome to offer me a country. *(to* MONALDESCHO) What do you want?

MONALDESCHO You were going it with the cloth.

CHRISTINA Tell me about Naples.

MONALDESCHO Not much revenue.

CHRISTINA The people?

MONALDESCHO Mostly thieves and scavengers, present company excepted.

CHRISTINA Fancy yourself, do you?

MONALDESCHO Why not, I'm Neapolitan. Good family. We'd be a popular alliance, you and I.

CHRISTINA We'll see.

MONALDESCHO He's a good looking fellow. *She turns in enquiry* The Cardinal.
She turns away, he pursues her.
I'm your man. I'm loyal.

CHRISTINA True. Very well, come if it pleases you.

MONALDESCHO In command of the army?

CHRISTINA *I* shall be in command of the army. Oh, don't sulk man, we'll see you get something out of it. Why not play the cards dealt – why not? I was a queen, I'll be a queen again, at least I've the training for it.

MONALDESCHO And the rest of us get our rewards in heaven, eh?

CHRISTINA What are you complaining of, you're good-looking!

MONALDESCHO Plenty of plain women aren't Queen of Sweden.

She clouts him.

Is *he* coming? The Cardinal?

CHRISTINA Perhaps. So don't get too ambitious.

She goes.

MONALDESCHO Why you, you hump-backed mare? Why you? Why not me?

SCENE FIVE

Action

Enter AZZOLINO, cloaked, followed by a CAPTAIN of the Queen's guard.

CAPTAIN	Welcome back, sir, your presence has been much missed.
AZZOLINO	I wish my news was good. How goes it in the field?
CAPTAIN	Badly. Our formations are too well known. We suspect a traitor.
AZZOLINO	Where is the Marchese?
CAPTAIN	In bed sir. He is not himself.
AZZOLINO	And the Queen? We heard of the sad death of her mother.
CAPTAIN	Alas, yes sir.

CHRISTINA *enters.*

CHRISTINA	You're back, why weren't we told?
AZZOLINO	I was on my way to pay my respects to you. I am so distressed to hear of your loss.
CHRISTINA	Eh?
AZZOLINO	Her Majesty, your mother.
CHRISTINA	Oh who cares, she's not important. A foolish woman.
AZZOLINO	Perhaps the simple suffer less.
CHRISTINA	Not her .. always in pain or a rage – miserable life.
AZZOLINO	She bred you.
CHRISTINA	I bolted!
AZZOLINO	We all fail our parents.
CHRISTINA	Not at all, you're a Cardinal.
AZZOLINO	But I am not the Pope. Be comforted. I must speak with you privately. *(The* CAPTAIN *goes)* There is a traitor in the camp.
CHRISTINA	By God there is! We marched east after you left us, they were waiting. When we broke out

	across the river, the Spaniards were there in force. Our troops tired and we are without reserve.
AZZOLINO	And you have no knowledge of who has betrayed you?
CHRISTINA	None.
AZZOLINO	Then I am the bearer of ill news.
CHRISTINA	Who? His name.
AZZOLINO	The Marchese.
CHRISTINA	No, no, that's impossible, you're mistaken.
AZZOLINO	There can be no error.
CHRISTINA	He's my man! I'm in his interest!
AZZOLINO	My Lady, I have proof. There is a letter. You will recognise the handwriting.
CHRISTINA	No. I won't believe it. He must be killed at once.
AZZOLINO	No.
CHRISTINA	*(calls)* Fetch Monaldescho!
AZZOLINO	You must remain within the law! It is as vital politically that you do nothing in haste as it is vital for your soul that you do nothing in anger.
CHRISTINA	Oh don't codge me, Pope's man. Where is he?

The CAPTAIN *returns with* MONALDESCHO, *who throws himself at* CHRISTINA'S *feet. A* SOLDIER *stands by to cut off* MONALDESCHO'S *retreat.*

CHRISTINA	Why? Why? *(she kicks him)* What's the matter, lost your tongue – don't worry, you soon will!
MONALDESCHO	Highness .. Highness .. please ...
CHRISTINA	Recognise this? No wonder you've been stinking the place out! Think I don't know your ignorant hand?

AZZOLINO It must be exposed to the process of law!

CHRISTINA What was it, money? You've bled us white for your pretty face! Kill him.

AZZOLINO No! At least confess him first!

CHRISTINA Do it then.

MONALDESCHO *(clinging to the* CARDINAL'S *legs)* Save me .. please ... please ... please ....

AZZOLINO My son, you must make your confession.

MONALDESCHO No, I don't want to die ... save me. don't let them kill me .. father .. father ...

CHRISTINA Get on with it!

AZZOLINO Majesty, he will not confess, he asks me to intercede for him.

CHRISTINA Oh, do what you please. Take him away.

MONALDESCHO *breaks free, falls at her feet. He kisses her skirt, clinging to it, and babbling.*

MONALDESCHO Madonna, madonna .... I love you ...

CHRISTINA What!

MONALDESCHO I love you .. I love you ... I love you ...

CHRISTINA Kill him!

And she snatches the dagger from the CAPTAIN *and strikes* MONALDESCHO *in the throat. He gurgles, gasps, and is silent.* AZZOLINO *kneels by the body, praying.*

CHRISTINA Not so pretty now. Remove the carcass.

The SOLDIERS *take the body off.*

CHRISTINA Perhaps now you will take me seriously.

AZZOLINO But I have always done so.

CHRISTINA Why do you look like that?

AZZOLINO   I am frightened, madam.
CHRISTINA   Are we all to be like you .. hiding from life in a woman's skirts?
AZZOLINO   The act was barbaric.
CHRISTINA   Help me.

He bows slightly and goes. The CAPTAIN *enters.*

CHRISTINA   Has he gone?
CAPTAIN   Ma'am?
CHRISTINA   The Cardinal.
CAPTAIN   Yes, ma'am.
CHRISTINA   Fetch him back. I am ill.
CAPTAIN   Shall I call the leech, ma'am?
CHRISTINA   Fetch him back. No. Give him a bowl of cherries.
CAPTAIN   Ma'am?
CHRISTINA   Who's that? Is someone there? And tell them I won't sign – you can cry your eyes out, just remember that. You know who you're speaking to?
CAPTAIN   Ma'am? *(He approaches)*
CHRISTINA   No you don't, you don't catch me .. oh no, no, no. *(Brisk)* I'll take a hot bath now. *(Goes, abruptly)*

The CAPTAIN *stands, amazed.*

SCENE SIX

Dolls

CHRISTINA, *in a dressing gown and cap, seated. She is immobile, hands in lap.* LUCIA *enters.*

LUCIA   Majesty?

No response. LUCIA *sighs.*

> Your favourite bonbons, from the Contessa! No? *(She puts them on* CHRISTINA'S *lap and tidies her, sighing)* You must eat! If you don't eat you will die and what will become of us?

She goes. A pause.

ANGELICA, LUCIA'S *daughter, enters, carrying her dolls. She notices the sweets, and takes one. Then she feeds her dolls the sweets.*

ANGELICA   Say please. Good girl. Please ... good girl. Eat up. Be good.

She pushes a sweet into CHRISTINA'S *mouth. Seeing that she does not eat it, she slaps her lightly on the hand.*

> Naughty girl. Eat up .. eat up.

CHRISTINA *starts to cry silently, her face contorting.*

Very naughty! Stop crying! *(She slaps* CHRISTINA *on the hand. Then, tiring of the game, she picks up her dolls to go .. pauses, puts another sweet into* CHRISTINA'S *hand)*

Eat up. *(She goes)*

CHRISTINA *slowly turns her head after the child, then slowly begins to eat.*

SCENE SEVEN

A Visitor

LUCIA *enters with flowers, returns with wine, followed by* ANGELICA, *with ribbons in her hair.*

CHRISTINA *is sitting in her chair, but is wearing an overgarment in pink, festively decorated.*

CHRISTINA	The paintings .. you don't think they might be too –
LUCIA	No, no, madonna .. he is a man of the world.
CHRISTINA	Of course. And the porco alla Romana?
LUCIA	Will be to perfection.

LUCIA *bobs and she and the child go.*
CHRISTINA *moves about restlessly. She opens a book, puts it down, picks up a glass, picks up a whip from the sidetable and plays with it, puts it down. She sits with the book, arranging her skirt.*

LUCIA *enters.* CHRISTINA *leaps to her feet, dropping the book.*

LUCIA   Majesty, he is here!

CHRISTINA *nods, then gets on her hand and knees, looking for the book.*

AZZOLINO *enters, looks about.*

· **CHRISTINA** *(from the floor)* Oh, there you are. Please, be seated.

Pause.

AZZOLINO   *(soft)* You are well?
CHRISTINA   Much better, much better. How long are you in Rome?
AZZOLINO   His Holiness feels that –
CHRISTINA   We had a letter. Perhaps you should read it. As you see, we are allowed to meet. So long as we don't touch the body. Not much chance of that. *(She smiles. Pause)* You didn't come.
AZZOLINO   It was forbidden.
CHRISTINA   Would you have come?
AZZOLINO   I was so pleased to get your letters. You are, as always, superbly informed.
CHRISTINA   I know how you hate being out of Rome. And now you're here. On Vatican orders. What is your mission?
AZZOLINO   *(produces papers)* The suggestion that Your Majesty be offered the throne of Poland –
CHRISTINA   I've refused it.
AZZOLINO   The offer is a secure one.

CHRISTINA   I have no choice. This room is now my whole
             world. To go as far as that door fills me with
             terror. I can no more step into the street than
             fly from the rooftops. It seems I am to be a
             prisoner for the rest of my life. So, as you see, I
             need a friend.
AZZOLINO   It will pass.
CHRISTINA   *(throws herself at his feet)* Please, I am in
             torment! How may I be absolved? I took his
             life for mere temper – not even necessity,
             conviction.
AZZOLINO   My dear friend.

He lifts her. She holds on to him.

CHRISTINA   Say you forgive me .. say you forgive me.
             Don't leave me, say you will stay, they will let
             you stay .. please, please stay .. I need you!
AZZOLINO   You must find a way to forgive yourself.
CHRISTINA   No, please. You know what I want.
AZZOLINO   My daughter .. pray.
CHRISTINA   I beg you. I've waited. I've been patient.

She makes to embrace him. He steps back.

AZZOLINO   *(gently)* I think I must now withdraw.
CHRISTINA   Oh. You're afraid. There have been women.
             Why not me? Oh, what am I but the bag of
             excrement that St. Bernard would have all
             women? Please.
AZZOLINO   *(low)* You must understand. There can be
             nothing. Nothing at all.
CHRISTINA   I agree. Your presence .. that's all I ask –

LUCIA *enters.*

LUCIA   Madonna .. madonna ... quickly .. my child ..
                she is choking!
CHRISTINA   *(howls)* Angelica! *(She rushes from the room,*
                followed by LUCIA *and* AZZOLINO *)*

Pause. Enter AZZOLINO *and* CHRISTINA. *She stops short.*

CHRISTINA   I left the room!
AZZOLINO   Yes.
CHRISTINA   Why are you smiling?
AZZOLINO   You saved the child's life!
CHRISTINA   Nonsense, I gave her a fine blow in the
                stomach!

They laugh, stimulated by the success of the rescue.

                How flimsy rank is. In human need it dissolves
                at once. So warm down there! The smell of
                ironed clothes .. linen .. lace –
                Food ... baking ...
                And babies. The smell of babies. I like the
                smell of babies – can that be wrong?

AZZOLINO   Of course not.
CHRISTINA   Does it take so many – I was never in a kitchen
                before.
AZZOLINO   They are proud and happy to be in your
                service.
CHRISTINA   Why?
AZZOLINO   You are a Queen.
CHRISTINA   A hundred servants, to wait on one woman?
                Can that be right? Why do we prey on one
                another – we should all be on the same footing.
AZZOLINO   These thoughts are valuable. And can be
                fruitfully employed.

CHRISTINA   *(drily)* Poland, you mean?

AZZOLINO   Can it be wrong to bring peace and prosperity to an unhappy land?

CHRISTINA   Peace in Poland? You are disingenuous or naive.

AZZOLINO   I do not deny the instability of Poland's borders.

CHRISTINA   No. There'll be no more killing.

AZZOLINO   Even if the cause be just?

CHRISTINA   I have *BEEN* as a man. I have commanded. I have signed death warrants, consigned regiments to the sword. All done in my name. I have even committed murder. What more do you want?

AZZOLINO   We live in an imperfect world.

CHRISTINA   Oh, be your own man .. for once! I look at you and your eyes are made of lint, and so you can sit there and send me to hell. In the name of our friendship, what sort of man are you?

AZZOLINO   I am ashamed. I know you suffer – have suffered.

CHRISTINA   Must it always be the sword? By God, half the world are women .. they've learned subversion, to keep their teeth in their mouths and the rope off their backs, why not try that?

AZZOLINO   Alas, are women free? I speak to you as to a man who has been a king but who, as a woman, has that compassion not only to save the life of a child but to respond to the poor and needy, those in your own service, who, I may say, are as Croesus compared with the poor devils of Cracow under the yoke.

CHRISTINA   Yet who are the poorest of all? Women, children .. the old. Are they the fighters, the creators of war? You say you want me for the fight, and, it's true, I was bred as a man, despising the weakness of women. I begin to question the favour. To be invited to join the killing, why, where's the advantage? Half the world rapes and destroys – must the women, the other half, join in?

AZZOLINO It's a pretty point.

CHRISTINA Pretty?

AZZOLINO Peace and human dignity are not to be guarded without cost.

CHRISTINA Guarded from what? From whom? I speak not only of the battlefield. I have been in the courtroom and sat through the cases of murder, and robbery with violence. Who does this – the women? I begin to see that I have been a traitor to my sex – oh, I believed, when I commanded an army, that I fought for the weak and helpless. We fought for land! And the conscripted men got none of it, poor devils .. ripped away from their fields – for I don't condemn every man as a murdering brute, far from it, or we'd not have survived this far. But when I think of it .. young men destroyed, infants burned in their cradles.. women violated ... how wrong, how wrong I have been to condemn women for their weakness ... they have kept us alive!

AZZOLINO No-one denies this. We revere the mother. We depend on her .. on her love.

CHRISTINA But there is no respect. Only power is respected. Who respects slavery, the dispossessed? A women acquiesces in her slavery, and why? For the chains of her own flesh ... blood, bone, sinew! We should listen to them! They know how to share rather than take .. by God, they share their very bodies with their own young, with us! They give. And we think nothing of it.

AZZOLINO   Do not the Scriptures tell us .. the meek shall inherit the earth?

CHRISTINA   But you still want me for Queen-General of Poland. No. No more killing. I begin to perceive that I am a woman. What that is, heaven knows .. the philosopy is yet to be written, there is a world to be explored.

AZZOLINO   A world without action?

CHRISTINA   *(shows him a plate she has been playing with)* Beautiful, don't you think? From San Bernardino. So blue. But the dye was poisonous, it killed the potters who used it. Until one day they put down their brushes, all of them. The Count was powerless, he had not the skills himself. The blue is softer now, not so angry.

I never saw the nature of it. Women submit, not from weakness, but for love.

I have been betrayed.

This ... *(she slaps her abdomen)* ... this has been betrayed.

AZZOLINO   You are upset. It is the accident with the child, it has distressed you. Do not distress yourself. Be calm.

CHRISTINA   You are afraid that I shall be hysterical? Yes, I too have despised hysterical women.

You want me, all of you, as a man. You will allow me in ... as your confederate ... to suit your purposes —

AZZOLINO   But you are magnificent! Think what you could not do for Poland! Poland can give you the power to contribute ... with meaning ... to extend yourself. A new purpose.

CHRISTINA   *(pause)* And can Poland give me a child?

AZZOLINO   Christina ... *(helplessly)* ... if you see that as your function —

CHRISTINA   Why not? Why must I make apology, or prove my case? It is my nature. True, in my case an alternative has been offered — I have been offered the choice of an active life. In God's name, why must I choose?

AZZOLINO   You could have married.

CHRISTINA   And been denied my mind.

AZZOLINO   But that is nature.

CHRISTINA   Nature is us! We are nature! It is we who change and create change! If you want my mind, then you must take my body. I see it so clearly now. I have been denied my birthright. I have been denied the very centre of myself. Why is it so warm down there? Why is it so cold here?

Silence.

AZZOLINO   So your answer to Poland is no.

CHRISTINA   Cannot you give me a child?

AZZOLINO   Christina, please .. !

CHRISTINA   Is that so bizarre?

AZZOLINO   I beg you ...

CHRISTINA What would it cost you? I'm a woman, Decio, and I've no-one to weep for.

AZZOLINO My dear, you have had a whole country. And could have, a second time.

CHRISTINA They were not my children. She can weep, she has some-one to weep for. Look at me, my eyes are dry. I have nothing. You offer me the whole world – for nothing. The privilege of action ... at the cost of oneself. What sort of bargain is that?

AZZOLINO But we must all submit to circumstance –

CHRISTINA Why? Why should we? What are you, a fool or a liar, I shall beat you up in a minute.

AZZOLINO Christina ..

CHRISTINA Look at me, what am I? I'm even beginning to grow a beard. I'm to be what I'd have given half my life for once – I'm to be a man!

AZZOLINO Christina, stop it, you're becoming unreasonable!

She picks up the whip and slashes at him spitefully. He grapples for it, then dodges round the table. She chases him, half laughing, half crying.

Christina, stop it, you're getting excited.

CHRISTINA I want my children. Where are they ... where are my children?

AZZOLINO Christina..

CHRISTINA Where's my daughter, where's my son, you've cheated me, all of you!

AZZOLINO Now stop it .. ow!

CHRISTINA Don't tell me what I can have if I fight. I won't fight. I won't fight, I tell you, I won't fight! If you want arms and legs to blow up, make them yourself. I want my children, do you hear .. I want my children. *(She flops down, and begins to cry)* I want my children and I won't fight. I won't fight, I tell you – I won't fight!

She catches him with a slash as he skirts round the table. He reverses quickly and she strikes at him again.

AZZOLINO Not on the face, Christina, not on the face!
CHRISTINA I won't fight.

They are both breathless.

AZZOLINO Pax .. pax – then what will you do? *(He is breathless)* What can be achieved without it?
CHRISTINA Oh you fool – everything. *(ecstatic)* Everything! Everything, you fools .. everything!

She approaches him, dropping the whip. She embraces him.

(mood change) Everything .... oh please ....

She reaches up to kiss him. And he flinches away from her.

CHRISTINA *becomes hysterical.* LUCIA *enters quickly. She and the* CARDINAL *confer, she shakes a hand, as to indicate not to interfere.*

AZZOLINO Is she often like this?
CHRISTINA I can hear you, you know.

CHRISTINA *recovers.*

AZZOLINO You are recovered?

CHRISTINA   I am well.

She crosses, to exit at a distance.

                        You must come and see my new library. Volumes you won't find anywhere else.

AZZOLINO   I look forward to that.

CHRISTINA   Till our next meeting then.

She blows her nose loudly on her skirt, and goes.

LUCIA   My poor lady.

AZZOLINO   We are indebted to you for your loving care.

LUCIA   Thank you, father.

AZZOLINO   A great, brave women. Fine intellect.

LUCIA   Learned.

AZZOLINO   And caring.

LUCIA   Indeed. We are all in her debt.

AZZOLINO   I echo that.

LUCIA   *(sighs)* Nothing to look at, of course. *(She pats her hair)*

They exchange a smile and exit.